SUMMARY:

Atomic Habits – An Easy & Proven Way to Build Good Habits & Break Bad Ones

by James Clear

Essential Insight Summaries

TABLE OF CONTENTS

BOOK ABSTRACT

In this book, James Clear introduces a four-step model for every human behavior.

Cue, Craving, Response, Reward. He does not only provide a well detailed description on how to create habits, he also gives an outstanding insight about human behavior.

A craving is created when meaning is assigned a cue. The brain begins to construct an emotion or feeling to describe the current situation, which indicates that a craving can only take place when there is an opportunity.

When a cue is observed without a desire to change state that means the individual is content with the situation. The first step in any behavior is observation, craving seeks to fix everything.

Observation without craving is to realize the need of not fixing everything. If an individual does not crave a change in state, the mind does not generate a problem to be solved. If motivation and desire are great enough, actions will be taken no matter how difficult it is. The trick to doing anything is first cultivating a desire for it.

Every emotion is an emotional decision at some level. Whatever the reason for action, emotions compel action. The feeling comes first then the behavior. Our thoughts and actions are rooted in what appeals to us not necessarily what is logical. That is the reason why appealing to people's emotions is stronger than appealing to reason.

When people are emotional they rarely appeal to reason. Action will always reveal motive. Response always precedes reward. The reward only comes after the energy has been expelled.

Failing to achieve something when desire is high is more painful than failing to achieve something when we don't think much about it in the first place.

The first law of behavior change is to make it obvious. The two most common cues are time and location. A habit is likely to occur when it is paired with time and location. New habits can be paired with existing habits through habit stacking. The second law of behavior change is to make it attractive. The more attractive the opportunity is the more likely it is to be habit-forming.

Habits are a dopamine-driven feedback loop. When dopamine rises, so does the motivation to actually take action. The anticipation of a reward gets individuals to take action. The greater the anticipation, the greater the dopamine spike. Temptation building is one way to make habits more attractive by pairing what is wanted with what is needed. The third law is to make it easy. The most efficient form is learning to practice than planning.

Individuals must focus on action and not being in motion. Behavior can become more automatic through repetition. The amount of time it takes to perform a habit is not important as the number of times it is done.

The fourth law is to make it satisfying. We are more likely to repeat a behavior when the experience is satisfying. The human brain has evolved to prioritize immediate reward over delayed reward. To get a habit to stick, you need to feel immediately successful even in a small way.

Anyone can work hard when they feel motivated. The ability to keep going when work isn't exciting that makes the difference. Reflection and review process allow an individual to remain conscious of your performance over time.

The tighter an individual clings to an identity, the harder it becomes to grow beyond it. Each improvement eventually is like adding a grain of sand to the positive side of the scale, slowly tilting things in your favor, if you stick with it long enough, you'll hit a tipping point.

ABOUT THE AUTHOR

James Clear is an author, travel photographer, and entrepreneur. He is the author of "Atomic Habits," and the creator of Habits Academy.

He enjoys weightlifting and spends most of his time on his blog JamesClear.com

His writing is focused on how better habits can be created, how humans can harness and develop their potential and live better lives, as he combines ideas from several fields which include Neuroscience, Psychology, Philosophy, Biology, and many more.

With the latest scientific research and findings, he reveals how people can improve the quality of their lives by focusing on behavior and the data behind high performance.

His work has been covered by several media outlets, including The New York Times, Entrepreneur, TIME, and others.

IMPORTANT NOTE ABOUT THIS BOOK

At Essential Insight Summaries, we pride ourselves in providing key points in life-changing books in the shortest amount of time. Our summaries focus on bringing vital information that enhances your knowledge and understanding, in a specific subject matter. We focus on the essentials, to ensure you maximize knowledge in the shortest possible time.

This comprehensive summary is based on *Atomic Habits: An Easy & Proven Way to Build Good Habits & Break Bad Ones* by James Clear and does not share any affiliation with the author or original work in any way or form. The summary does not utilize any text from the original work. We want our readers to use this summary as a study companion to the original book, and not as a substitute.

THE FUNDAMENTALS

WHY TINY CHANGES MAKE A BIG DIFFERENCE

CHAPTER 1

THE SURPRISING POWER OF ATOMIC HABITS

For over 110 years, no British cyclist ever won the cycling event in cycling's biggest race, Tour de France. Professional cyclists had endured over a century of mediocrity and shame.

A top manufacturer in Europe had been reported to have not sold bikes to the British team because it may affect sales if other professional teams saw Brits using their gear.

Brailsford was hired to put British cycling on a new trajectory. He had a relentless commitment to a philosophy of searching for the smallest margin of improvement in everything he did, and this was quite peculiar to him.

He began to work tirelessly with his coaches. They made new designs for the bike seats. Used biofeedback sensors to monitor how athletes responded to workouts. They had the team test several fabrics and racing suits. They tested several fast, muscle-recovery gels, several adjustments were made and results began rushing in faster than anyone would have thought possible.

They won over sixty percent of the gold medals available in the road and track cycling events at the 2008 Olympics, barely five years after Brailsford took over. In four years, they set nine Olympic records and seven world records.

Bradley Wiggins won the Tour de France for the first time in history. He won four more times in six years. They won one hundred seventy-eight world championships and sixty-six Olympic or Paralympic gold medals and five Tour de France in ten years.

WHY SMALL HABITS MAKE A BIG DIFFERENCE

Most times many people seem convinced that massive success requires massive action; nothing could be further from the truth. Yes, one percent improvement isn't particularly notable but can be far more meaningful, most especially, over time. If anyone can improve one percent each day, he will be thirty-seven times better than he was, but if he declines one percent daily he will decline nearly to zero.

ONE PERCENT BETTER EVERY DAY

Habits are a compound interest of self-improvement. The effect of any habit can multiply if they are repeated. The impact may not be seen immediately but will be months or years after, and it can be enormous. This slow pace transformation is the unfortunate reason why many bad habits slide; eating unhealthy meals, ignoring family members. A single decision is usually easy to dismiss. A small change to daily habits can guide a man's life to a different destination, success is usually a product of daily habits. Many people are concerned about the result in their lives than they are about their current trajectory, it should be by far, the reverse.

Results in life are a measure of habits, the net worth of anyone is just a lagging measure of their financial habits so is anyone's knowledge, weight or Health, you usually get what you repeat. If you want to predict where you'll end up in life follow the curve of your daily choices, time magnifies the margin between success and failure, it will multiply whatever you feed it. Bad habits can cut a man down just as easily as a good habit can build up, this is why this understanding is crucial and how you can design them to your advantage.

WHAT PROGRESS IS REALLY LIKE

Moments of breakthrough are usually as a result of many previous actions, which in turn builds up the potential to unleash a major change, in order to make meaningful, difference habits to persist long enough. Mastery requires a great deal of patience. If you do the same thing long enough, then success is sure. The outside world may call it an overnight success but it will be clear it is a product of long, daily, and consistent work.

THE PLATEAU OF LATENT POTENTIAL

Every habit has its seed in a single decision. All big things usually come from small beginnings. Every decision that is repeated, sprouts a habit which becomes stronger. Usually the task of breaking a habit is more difficult than cultivating a new one.

FORGET ABOUT GOALS, FOCUS ON SYSTEM INSTEAD

Many people who claim mastery over habits and behavior will say the best way to achieve the best results in life is to set actionable goals, but really? Is it?

Results actually have very little to do with goal setting and more to do with the system followed. Goals are all about the result a man sees but systems would describe the process followed.

For example, an entrepreneur's goal may be to build a million-dollar company. The system would describe his marketing campaign, how he runs his product ideas, and how he hires employees.

Anyone will still get results if they ignored the goals and focused on the system, as the only way to actually succeed is to get better each day.

Goals are important for direction but systems are more important for real progress. We will see that successful and unsuccessful people most times have the same goals so that can't be where the difference lies. Reaching a goal will only produce a momentary win. This mindset immediately sets the happiness into another future expectation and achievement.

If the process, rather than the product is loved, happiness would no longer be in the future since it's no longer about getting a result. Usually the purpose of setting a goal is to achieve and the purpose of building a system is to continue achieving. Eventually only commitment to the process will determine progress.

A SYSTEM OF ATOMIC HABITS

We don't usually rise to the level of our goals but we will always fall to the level of our systems. Habits are like atoms, each one has a fundamental unit that contributes to the overall improvement. They are a component of the system of compound growth; the building blocks of results. They usually are a small change, a marginal gain, or minute percentage improvement which may seem too small to be significant but soon build on each other and multiply to a great degree which would eventually surpass the initial cost of investment.

CHAPTER 2

HOW YOUR HABITS SHAPE YOUR IDENTITY

(AND VICE VERSA)

Most times it feels like quite difficult to keep a good over a bad habit. Habits, like exercise or meditation, seem reasonable for a few days then become a real hassle. Most habits prove challenging to change because many people try to change it the wrong way. People usually try to change the wrong things.

THREE LAYERS OF BEHAVIOR CHANGE

There are three layers at which any change can occur.

The first, is the change in outcomes, usually concerned with changing results like losing weight. It is usually about what is gained.

The second, is the change in process. Concerned with changing systems and habits like implementing a new routine at the gym, usually associated with what is done.

The third, which is considered the deepest is changing identity. The view of the world, self-image and judgement, identity is about what is believed.

Every system of action has behind it a system of beliefs. For instance, the system of democracy is founded on beliefs like majority rule, freedom, and social equality unlike dictatorship where there is strict obedience and total authority.

It is hard to change any habit without changing the underlying belief systems. In trying to change a habit, a man must be proud about a particular aspect of his identity which will bring motivation to maintain habits associated with the identity. Any behavior change is an identity change as behaviors are a direct reflection of identity. This is because people's action will align with their belief in a particular aspect of their identity. Identity change is a great force for self-improvement; to become the best version of ourselves we must continually edit our beliefs.

THE TWO-STEP PROCESS TO CHANGING YOUR IDENTITY

Every belief a man has was not inborn, it was learned and conditioned through experience. The more a behavior is repeated the more reinforced the identity associated with that behavior becomes. The more evidence there is for a belief system, the strongly it is believed.

Frequency of habits will exhibit a man's identity, so it will not be improper to call a man's identity his "repeated beingness." No one just changes by simply deciding to be someone entirely new. Change occurs bit by bit, day after day, a microevolution taking place. This process of building habits is the process of becoming or having an identity.

So, the very practical way to change who we are is to alter what we do, by proving to ourselves in small wins we can change ourselves to that image we see in our head. Once a person has settled what and who he wants to be then he can begin to take small steps to reinforcing that identity as habits shape identity and vice versa.

THE REAL REASON HABITS MATTER

Habits can help anyone achieve anything but habits are fundamentally not about achieving but becoming. They matter because they can help anyone become the person he wants to be. The deepest belief of a person can be developed through these channels. A man would eventually become his habits!

CHAPTER 3

HOW TO BUILD BETTER HABITS IN 4 SIMPLE STEPS

An experiment conducted in 1898 by Edward Thorndike, would essentially lay the foundation for habits formation and rules that guide behavior. By studying cats, placing them in a device he called puzzle box, where the cat can escape through a door by pulling at a loop of chord, pressing a lever, or stepping on a platform.

He then tracked the behavior of the cats through many trials as they moved randomly, initially looking for a means to escape then magically performing an act that flung the door open, gradually all the cats learned to associate the act of pressing a lever to the reward of escaping from the box. After about twenty trials, the behavior became so automatic that the cats escaped within seconds.

This outstanding study describes the learning process and will provide a perfect starting point for understanding habit formation as it established that behaviors that are followed by positive consequences tend to be repeated while those that produce negative consequences are less likely to be repeated.

WHY YOUR BRAIN BUILDS HABITS

A habit is any behavior whose repetition has caused it to become automatic. Most times when people encounter a new situation, the brain will have to choose as to how to respond to it.

This process of habit formation is usually a product of trial and error. At this moment, there's a lot of neurological activity going on in the brain. The brain is busy trying to understand the most effective course of action. As habits are created and reinforced, the level of activity in the brain decreases. There's usually not much needed to analyze so much anymore. The brain immediately skips the trial and error process to create a mental rule. If this is this that has to be that, which is as a result of experience.

This results in the brain always working to preserve conscious attention for essential task. Building habits in the present allows a person to do more of what he wants to do in the future.

THE SCIENCE OF HOW HABITS WORK

The process involved in habit building can be classified into four steps:

Cue: this is a bit of information that predicts a reward like sex or approval. It triggers the brain to initiate a behavior. The mind continually analyzes the internal and external environment for any clue of the location of reward; they lead naturally to craving.

Craving: this differs from person to person. They are that motivational force behind every habit. It is not the habit that is craved for but the feeling of relief or satisfaction that activity brings. It is closely linked to a desire to change the internal state. Feelings, emotions, or thoughts are what transforms cue to craving as cues is meaningless in themselves until they are interpreted.

Response: habits performed are referred to as the response. Degree of motivation usually determine response. If an action requires more energy or effort, whether physical or mental, that a person is willing to expend then he won't do it. Response depends on ability and it delivers the reward.

Reward: this usually is the end point of every habit; the cue is about observing the reward; the craving is about wanting a reward; and the response is about obtaining the reward. Reward satisfies craving. It teaches which actions are worth remembering in the near future.

If any behavior is insufficient, it won't become a habit. Without the cue, the habit will not even start. If the craving is reduced, there won't be enough motivation to take action. If the behavior is made difficult, it won't be done either. Also, if the result doesn't satisfy the desire, it won't be repeated.

THE HABIT LOOP

The cue always triggers craving, which motivates a response. Then a reward is provided, satisfying the craving and ultimately becomes affiliated with the cue.

All these steps form a major neurological feedback loop, known as the habit loop. As every behavior is driven by a desire to solve a particular problem, this can be divided in to two phases: the problem phase, which includes the cue and craving; and solution phase, which includes the response and reward. For instance:

PROBLEM PHASE

Cue: Your phone buzzes with a new text message.

Craving: You want to learn the contents of the message.

SOLUTION PHASE

Response: You grab your phone and read text message.

Reward: You satisfy craving to read the message. Grabbing your phone becomes associated with your phone buzzing.

Many people in their adult lives barely notice the habits that run their lives. After decades of mental programming, everyone automatically slips into a pattern of thinking and acting.

THE FOUR LAWS OF BEHAVIOR CHANGE

These laws can be seen as a lever that influences human behavior. When those levers are in the right place, creating a good habit is effortless. However, when in the wrong place, it's almost impossible.

HOW TO CREATE A GOOD HABIT

1st Law (Cue): Make it obvious.

2nd Law (Craving): Make it attractive.

3rd Law (Response): Make it easy.

4th Law (Reward): Make it satisfying.

HOW TO BREAK A BAD HABIT (INVERSE OF THE LAWS)

1st Law (Cue): Make it invisible.

2nd Law (Craving): Make it unattractive.

3rd Law (Response): Make it difficult.

4th Law (Reward): Make it unsatisfying.

These laws apply to nearly every field. They can be used no matter what the challenge is. There is no need for completely different strategies for each habit.

Understanding these laws is the key to creating or breaking any habit. Habits are shaped by an individual's life systems.

THE 1ST LAW

MAKE IT OBVIOUS

CHAPTER 4

THE MAN WHO DIDN'T LOOK RIGHT

There was a story of a woman who had spent years working as a paramedic. When she arrived at an event and took one look at her father-in-law, she immediately noted the way he looked. Which was initially thought as a joke, but not until she insisted he had to go the hospital immediately.

A few hours later the man was undergoing lifesaving surgery, after an examination revealed he had blockage to a major artery and was at immediate risk of a heart attack; without his daughter-in-law's intuition he would have died.

How did she know? After many years of working with people with heart failure, she had unconsciously developed the ability to recognize this pattern on sight.

Many stories like this exist in the military; among analysts who can identify which blip on a radar screen is an enemy missile and which is a plane from their own fleet.

Museum curators discern the difference between an authentic piece of art and an expertly produced counterfeit, or hairdressers recognizing a pregnant woman by the feel of their hair.

The brain is a prediction machine. Most times when an experience is repeated, the brain observes what is important, sorts out details, and catalogues information for future use. The brain encodes lessons learned through experience. The brain and body can do a lot without thinking. This one, very surprising yet dangerous insight about habits: you don't need to be aware for a cue to begin.

As these habits form, actions come under the direction of the nonconscious and automatic mind, which will not be realized until the individual falls into old patterns. Before anyone can effectively build new habits, he needs to get a handle on the current ones; this can be very tasking. This is because once a habit is rooted in that person's life, it becomes unconscious and automatic, and can't be improved if it remains. Until the unconscious become conscious, it will direct a person's life and they will call it fate.

THE HABITS SCORECARD

The more automatic a behavior eventually becomes; the less likely people think about it. After doing something a thousand times before, it begins to lose value.

Many failures in performance are largely attributed to a lack of self-awareness. It could be very challenging for people to maintain awareness of what they actually do. The habits scorecard is a simple exercise anyone can use to become aware of their behavior.

All habits serve an individual in some way, even the bad habits. Habits that reinforce an individuals desired identity are usually good, while those that oppose desired identity are usually bad.

To create a habit scorecard, make a list of your daily activities; don't change anything at first. Observe your thoughts and actions without judgement or internal criticism. Don't praise or blame yourself, just be on the lookout for them. You can say them out loud. The aim is to make you more conscious of them. The usual process of every behavior change starts with awareness. The habit scorecard will help anyone recognize the habits and acknowledge the cues that trigger them, which then makes it possible for the individual to respond in the way that is beneficial to them.

CHAPTER 5

THE BEST WAY TO START A NEW HABIT

A group of researchers in Britain worked with two hundred forty-eight people to build better exercise habits over the course of two weeks.

The first group was asked to track how they exercised. The second was asked to track how they exercised but told to read on the benefits of exercise. The third received the same instruction as the second, however, were asked to plan for where and when the exercise was going to take place the following week.

The first and second group had about thirty-five to thirty-eight percent of people exercising, while the third had ninety-one percent exercising; double the normal rate.

This situation is what researchers refer to as implementation intention, which is a plan made beforehand as to when and where to act, and how a person intends to implement a particular habit. Implementation intentions from research, are effective for sticking with goals. They increase the odds that an individual will stick with habits. People who make a specific plan as to where and when an action will occur are more likely to follow through.

Any individual who gives a habit a time and a space to live in the world, will make the habit so obvious that an urge, with repetition, will always emerge to do what is right at the right time.

HABIT STACKING: A SIMPLE PLAN TO OVERHAUL YOUR HABITS

The Diderot Effect: the tendency one purchase to lead to another, came from the story of a French philosopher Denis Diderot, who lived almost his whole life in poverty until he had to pay for his daughter's wedding, which he couldn't afford as his being the co-founder and writer of Encyclopedia didn't pay all the bills.

The Empress of Russia, Catherine the Great, who loved books and enjoyed his Encyclopedia, heard of his financial trouble and bought his personal library for more than one hundred and fifty thousand dollars, which enabled him to pay for his daughter's wedding with money to spare.

He felt the urge to upgrade his possessions and one purchase led to another, leading to the next.

No behavior happens in isolation. Every behavior eventually becomes a cue that triggers the next behavior. An individual can use the interlinking nature of behavior to his advantage when it comes to building new habits.

Habit stacking is a special form of implementation intention. All an individual has to do to build new habits is to identify a current habit done daily and then stack this new behavior on top of it.

For example: Meditation. After I pour my cup of coffee each morning, I will meditate for one minute. The key is to tie a desired behavior to something already done daily. It can also be inserted in the middle of current routines.

This usually works best when the cue is highly specific and immediately actionable, specificity is important. The first law is to make it obvious. Implementation intentions and stacking are among the most reliable practical ways to design a clear plan for where and when to act.

CHAPTER 6

MOTIVATION IS OVERRATED; ENVIRONMENT OFTEN MATTERS MORE

From a research conducted at Massachusetts General Hospital in Boston, Anne Thorndike, a primary care physician believed she could improve the eating habits of thousands of hospital staff and visitors without changing their willpower or motivation in the slightest way. In fact, she didn't plan to talk to anyone.

They replaced soda with bottled water next to the food stations across the room, although soda was still in the primary refrigerator. Over the next three months, the number of bottled water sold increased by twenty-five point eight percent and that of soda dropped by eleven point four percent, similar adjustments were made to the food also and no one said a word to anyone.

People will always choose products not because of what they are but because of where they are. Environment is like an invisible hand that charts the course of human behavior. Despite unique personalities, under certain environmental conditions, certain behaviors tend to emerge.

That already shows that customers buy products because of the way they are presented to them much more than because they want them. The more available a product is the more likely an individual is to try them.

The most powerful of all sensory abilities in humans is vision. The human body contains almost eleven million sensory receptors and about ten million dedicated to sight alone.

Experts estimate that about half of the resources of the brain are dedicated to vision. It is, therefore, quite imperative to note that visual cues are the highest catalyst of behaviors. That is a small change in what is seen can lead to a big change in what is done. Thankfully we can design our environment to our advantage.

HOW TO DESIGN YOUR ENVIRONMENT FOR SUCCESS

Every habit is initiated by a cue, and individuals are more likely to observe cues that stand out. Most times, residential and work environments make habits difficult to do as there is no cue to trigger the behavior. For instance, it is easy not to practice the guitar when it's locked away in the closet with the key in the box upstairs. When the cues that spark up a habit are so subtle they are very easy to ignore.

However, creating visual cues could bring attention to a desired habit. If you want to make a habit a huge part of your life, make the cue a big part of your environment. By sprinkling triggers throughout your surroundings, the odds of thinking about the habit throughout the day will be increased.

Designing the environment to your advantage influences how we engage with our world. Most people live in a world that others have created for them. Environmental designs returns control to an individual and makes him the architect of his life.

THE CONTEXT IS THE CUE

Over time, habits become associated with the context surrounding a particular behavior. For example, many people drink more at parties among friends than they will ever drink alone.

Most times we mentally assign habits to locations of occurrence. Each location builds a connection to certain habits and routines. Behaviors are usually not defined by the objects in the environment but by relationship to them.

Anyone can train themselves to link a particular habit with a particular context. In a new environment habits can change easily, with this change the subtle triggers and cues in the present environment currently nudging can be altered.

It is usually easier to associate a new habit with a new context than to build a new habit in the face of a competing cue. When there is a mix of context, there will certainly be a mix of habits. For a stable and predictable behavior, there must be a stable and predictable environment. Therefore, a stable environment where everything has a proper place and purpose is an environment where habits can be formed easily.

CHAPTER 7

THE SECRET TO SELF-CONTROL

During the Vietnam War, it was discovered in a finding by a group of researchers that approximately thirty-five percent of the service members had tried heroin and as many as twenty percent were addicts. Lee Robins found out that when these heroin addicts returned home to their families, only about five percent of them became re-addicted within a year. These findings show that a radical change in the environment can cause addictions to dissolve spontaneously.

Soldiers in Vietnam spent all day around cues triggering heroin use: they had easy access to it, they had friends who were also addicts, and were constantly engulfed with the distress of war.

This finding opposes many cultural beliefs about bad habits. Addicts have been told they lack self-control. However, recent research reveals something different. As scientists analyze the findings, they discovered that people, who seem to have a high-level self-control spend less time in tempting situations.

It is easier to demonstrate self-restraint when you don't have to use it often. So, it's not by wishing to be a more disciplined person but by creating a more disciplined environment. Once a habit has been encoded, the urge to act follows whenever the environmental cues show up. No one consistently sticks to positive habits in a negative environment.

To dismiss a bad habit effectively, one has to do it from the source by reducing exposure to the cues that cause trigger it.

For example, if an individual can't get enough work done because of their phone, leave it in another room for a few hours.

This practice is the reverse of the first law: rather than make the cue visible, you make it invisible. Eradicate a single cue and the habit fades away. Therefore, self-control is temporal strategy. It could work once or twice then, boom, habit is back! Instead of resisting temptation whenever you desire to act right, design or optimize your immediate environment. Make the cues of the good habits very obvious and the cues of the bad invisible.

THE 2ND LAW

MAKE IT ATTRACTIVE

CHAPTER 8

HOW TO MAKE A HABIT IRRESISTIBLE

In the 1940s, Niko Tinbergen, a Dutch scientist, discovered an amazing pattern in some animals. For example, regarding the herring gull, the pecking of a red dot on the beak of adult gulls whenever newly hatched chicks wanted food. This red spot was replaced with fakes but they continued the same behavior as if they were genetically programmed that way; which got faster as the red spot increased in size.

Also, the graylag goose. The mother goose will roll back every egg that rolls out of the nest. The amazing discovery is that the goose seemed to roll back every round object; the bigger the object the greater the effect.

It appears like the brains of animals are programmed with certain behavioral rules, and when there seems to be an exaggerated version of that rule, it lights up.

These exaggerated cues are called supernormal stimuli by scientists. Humans are also prone to this exaggerated version of reality. For instance, when an individual doesn't know where his next meal is coming from he eats as much as he can; an excellent strategy for survival.

The primary role of food science is to develop food more attractive to consumers. Almost every food is enhanced in some ways; flavoring, crunchy, crispy, and creamy sensations. It keeps the eating experience interesting and novel, encouraging anyone to eat more.

So, scientist combined ingredients ultimately to make food more attractive. Therefore, the more attractive an opportunity is, the more likely it becomes habit forming. Society is filled with a highly doctored versions of reality. Advertisements are engineered with ideal lightening, photoshopped edits, exaggerating features to make them highly attractive. To increase the likelihood of a behavior occurring, simply make it attractive.

DOPAMINE-DRIVEN FEEDBACK LOOPS

Cravings can be tracked by scientists by measuring a neurotransmitter called Dopamine. Dopamine is very important to life. Without it, the ability to experience pleasure will remain, but the desire will be gone; thereby, inhibiting action.

Habits are dopamine-driven feedback loops. Every habit-forming behavior is associated with dopamine. It is released not only in the experience of pleasure, but at the anticipation of it. It is the anticipation of a reward—not fulfilment that gets us to act. Desire drives behavior, anticipation fuels action, and craving leads to the response. Since this is observed, temptation bundling strategy will be very helpful.

HOW TO USE TEMPTATION BUNDLING TO MAKE HABITS MORE ATTRACTIVE

Temptation bundling works when an individual links an action one wants with one he needs to do. Everyone will find a behavior attractive if it gets to be done with a favorite thing at the same time.

Premack's theory in psychology states that a more probable behavior will reinforce less probable behaviors. So, in doing the thing you need to do you do what you want to do too.

CHAPTER 9

THE ROLE OF FAMILY AND FRIENDS IN SHAPING HABITS

THE SEDUCTIVE PULL OF THE SOCIAL NORMS

Humans are herd animals. Everyone wants to fit in, to bond with others, and to earn the respect and approval of peers. Such inclinations are essential to survival.

One of the greatest human desires is to belong and this ancient preference exerts a strong influence on behavior. Most times, the customs and practices of life in society sweep humans along. People will always imitate the habits of the close, the many, and the powerful among them.

Proximity has a strong effect on behavior. People will usually copy the way closest people around them behave, even without realizing it. The closer a person is to another individual, the more likely he is to imitate his habits. We soak up the practices and qualities of those closest to us. One very effective thing to do to build better habits is to join a culture where your desired behavior is the normal behavior; new habits can be achieved when you see others doing them daily.

Individuals will look to groups whenever they are not sure how to act. There will be a constant scanning of the environment for clues as to how to behave. People check reviews from others to see how people feel about things before they go ahead. It is actually a smart strategy. There is evidence in numbers, but the normal behavior of the group will often overpower the desired behavior of the individual. If changing the habit is challenging to the tribe, change is usually not attractive. However, when change fits in to society then it's attractive and can be done easily.

Power, status, and prestige is the pursuit of every human. Everyone wants a medallion of some sort; to be praised, acknowledged, and recognized. The person with greater power and status has more resources, less worries, and proves to be more attractive mate. People are drawn to behaviors that earn them respect, approval, and admiration. That is why people are drawn to understanding the behavior of highly effective people. Many of our daily habits are imitations of the people we admire.

CHAPTER 10

HOW TO FIND AND FIX THE CAUSES OF YOUR BAD HABITS

WHERE CRAVINGS COME FROM

All behaviors are accompanied by a surface level craving and a deeper underlying motive. A craving is an appearance of a deep underlying motive. All habit-forming products do the same thing their predecessors do; they simply latch on to the desire to connect. Example Facebook: reduce stress and anxiety. Example YouTube: reduce uncertainty.

All habits seem to be modern day solutions to ancient desires. Habits are formed by associations; these associations determine whether a habit is predicted to be worth repeating or not. The brain is continuously absorbing information and observing cues in the environment. When an individual perceives a cue, the brain runs a simulation which predicts what to do in the next moment.

Behaviors are highly dependent on predictions. Life may feel reactive but it's actually predictive. Behaviors may come at an instant but they are preceded by predictions. The cause of all habits is the predictions that precede them.

A craving is a sense that something is incomplete. Desire is the difference between where an individual is and where he wants to be. The cravings from any individual and habits they perform are actually an attempt to address a fundamental underlying motive. When a habit successfully addresses a motive, the individual develops a craving to do it again. Habits become attractive when they are associated with positive feelings and can be used to our advantage rather than the reverse.

HOW TO REPROGRAM YOUR BRAIN TO ENJOY HARD HABITS

When hard habits are associated with positive experiences they become more attractive. Sometimes all an individual needs is a small shift of mindset. Reframing habits to highlight benefits rather than their drawbacks can reprogram the mind and make a habit seem more attractive.

For example:

Exercise: rather than say to yourself, "I need to go run in the morning," say, "It's time to build endurance and get really fast."

Finance: rather than see making money as sacrifice, see it as freedom. Realize that it is more of saving to increase your purchasing power than living below your current means to increase your future means.

Meditation: rather than distraction in meditation as making meditation frustrating see it as necessary to practice meditation, as it gives you a chance to catch your mind straying and practice returning to your breath.

These mindset shifts are not mystical. They really can help adjust the feelings you associate with a particular habit. You can also practice associating habits with something enjoyable, and that cue can come in handy when motivation is needed.

In reframing the associations an individual has about bad habits, he can find and fix the causes. In programing a prediction, anyone can transform a hard habit into a highly attractive one.

THE 3RD LAW

MAKE IT EASY

CHAPTER 11

WALK SLOWLY, BUT NEVER BACKWARD

A professor at the University of Florida, Jerry Uelsmann, made his film photography students work on a project to be submitted at the end of the semester.

He divided them in to two groups. The first group he explained, would be graded solely on "quantity" of pictures produced: one hundred photos graded an A, ninety photos graded a B, eighty graded a C, and so on. The second group would submit one photo and would be graded based on the "quality" of work produced.

At the end of the semester, the best photos were produced by the "quantity' group, this was because the honed their skill in the process of creating many photos and got better as they learned from their mistakes but the quality group sat down on one picture trying to make it perfect.

Many times, people are so focused on figuring out the best approach that they never get to take any action. There is a big difference between being in motion and taking action. People who are in motion are only planning and strategizing, good but not enough to get a result.

Those who act on the other hand will eventually get results. For example, it is not enough to want to be healthy by searching for better eating plans and reading books, that's motion. Sitting down to eat a good meal is the action. Motion is usually useful but not enough to get desired results.

To master any habit, you must learn to master the art of repetition not perfection.

HOW LONG DOES IT ACTUALLY TAKE TO FORM A NEW HABIT?

A behavior will become progressively automatic through repetition. This is the process of habit formation.

The more a person repeats an activity the more the brain restructures and connections in neurons are strengthened to become effective in that activity, this is called long-term potentiation.

Repetition is a form of change. Each time a habit is repeated a particular neural circuit associated with the habit is activated. These habits follow similar trajectory from effortful practice to automatic behavior, a process known as automaticity.

WALKING 10 MINUTES PER DAY

Most people stress themselves with how long it takes to form a new habit. The right focus should be "how long" does it take to make a repeated habit automatic. Time does not really matter. What actually matters is the rate of performing a particular habit as something could be done twice in thirty days and two hundred times. New habits usually require the same level of frequency. To build a habit, an individual must practice it and practice in ease.

CHAPTER 12

THE LAW OF LEAST EFFORT

THE SHAPE OF HUMAN BEHAVIOR

In his book, Jared Diamond explained how the difference in shape of continents has played a significant role in the spread of agriculture over the centuries. Farmers expanded along the east-west coast than along north-south, because they share the same latitude, they share the same climate.

Agriculture as a result, spread faster in Asia and Europe than America. This shows behavior change on a global scale. The real motivation in humans is to be lazy, so people will always follow opinions that require the least amount of work. People are motivated to do what is easy. Every action requires a certain amount of energy, the more energy it takes to occur the less likely it will. To enable a habit form, it must be easy; not to do easy things only but the less obstacle the more likely it is to occur.

HOW TO ACHIEVE MORE WITH LESS EFFORT

When voice-activated speakers emerged, products like Amazon echo, apple Home pod, and Google home became easier used.

A few years earlier having unlimited access to music was more of a frictionless activity than driving to a store to buy a CD. Many companies who have achieved success designed their products to eliminate and simplify many steps as much as they can. The major idea is to design an environment where building a habit is easy enough.

Much of the battle in establishing better habits over bad once is to find a way to increase obstacles associated with good habits and vice versa.

PRIME THE ENVIRONMENT FOR FUTURE USE

There are many ways to prime an environment so it's ready for immediate use. For instance, do you want to exercise? Set out your workout clothes, shoes, gym bag, and bottle water ahead. In doing that the good habit will have least resistance.

It is quite notable to see how less obstacles encountered prevent unwanted behavior. Whether the behavior change is as an individual or a parent, coach or leader, the question remains the same: "How can I redesign a world where this habit can be done easily?"

In redesigning your life, you will come to see how actions that matter most are also easiest to do.

CHAPTER 13

HOW TO STOP PROCRASTINATION BY USING THE TWO-MINUTE RULE

Habits are choices that influence conscious decisions which follow afterwards. It is usually easier to continue what you are already doing then start doing something entirely different.

Habits are like the entrance to a highway: they lead you through a part and not long after you are speeding down the next behavior. There are usually moments, daily, that deliver impactful, decisive moments. The moments between every choice, these are a fork in the road.

DECISIVE MOMENTS

These moments shape our choices. Options will always be subject to what is available. For instance, walking in to a restaurant will determine what will be eaten for launch and this is subject to what is on the menu list. Our limitations are where our habits lead us.

Although every day contains many moments, it is really a few choices that determine the path we take.

THE TWO-MINUTE RULE

The most effective way to avoid doing so much initially is to start small. Most habits can be brought down to two minutes. The idea is to make the habit as easy to start.

For instance, "Study for class," can become "Open my notes." "Do thirty minutes of yoga" can become" take out my yoga mat."

The major point is for the habit to show up because a habit has to be established first before it can be improved. When the basic skill of showing up is learned then there is hope to master more details. You have to standardize before you optimize. It is a mental trick. If you can master staying for two minutes, then you can master staying longer.

Start every habit convincing yourself it is just for two minutes. Strategies like this reinforce the identity you want to build. Almost all of life's goal can be transformed in to a two-minute behavior. Whenever there is a struggle to stick with a habit, you can employ the two-minute rule; a simple way to make habits easy.

CHAPTER 14

HOW TO MAKE GOOD HABITS INEVITABLE AND BAD HABITS IMPOSSIBLE

Now sometimes, success is more about making good habits hard not to perform. Make it difficult not to happen. If it is continually more struggle to follow through plans then you have to make it difficult by creating a commitment device. This helps you to make a choice in the present, which affects your action in the future.

Commitment devices enable you to take advantage of good intentions before you fall victim to temptation. For instance, to avoid further gambling sprees you can voluntarily ask to be added to the banned list. Commitment devices increase the odds that a good habit will occur by making bad habits difficult in the present.

HOW TO AUTOMATE A HABIT AND NEVER THINK ABOUT IT

The best way to break a bad habit is to make it impractical to do. Technology can transform actions that were once hard, annoying, and complicated into behaviors that are simple to perform.

When habits are handed over to technology you can have more time to do things that can't be automated. Technology creates a level of convenience that enables you to act on your smallest whims and desires.

When working in an individual's favor, automation can make good habits inevitable and bad habits impossible. It is the major way to lock in future behavior rather than relying on willpower in the moment.

THE 4TH LAW

MAKE IT SATISFYING

CHAPTER 15

THE CARDINAL RULE OF BEHAVIOR CHANGE

Most behaviors are likely to be repeated when the experiences are satisfying. This is quite logical. Pleasure teaches the brain that this behavior is worth remembering and repeating.

Successful companies understand this and make use of it. For example, toothpaste manufacturers enjoyed great success when they added mint to their products. In the same way, if an experience is not satisfying it may not be repeated next time, but much more than satisfaction, immediate satisfaction is what is needed.

THE MISMATCH BETWEEN IMMEDIATE AND DELAYED REWARDS

Many of the choices we make today will not be of immediate benefit. This is called a delayed reward environment because benefits of work only come after a while. Although there has been much change in the world, human nature has not changed. The way the brain evaluates rewards is inconsistent across time. We tend to value the present more than the future.

A reward available now is worth more than in the future. The consequences of bad habits are delayed while the rewards are immediate. That is why people will still smoke, knowing it increases the risk of cancer. Most times with bad habits, the immediate result is enjoyable but the ultimate outcome is bad; the reverse also for good habits. The cost of bad habits is in the future.

Most people understand that delaying immediate gratification is wise but still don't do it. The way to do this is to make those habits enjoyable.

HOW TO TURN INSTANT GRATIFICATION TO YOUR ADVANTAGE

The best way to get a habit to stick is to feel successful, even if it's in a small way. This feeling is a signal that the habit paid off and the work was worth the effort.

Reinforcement ties habit to an immediate reward, which makes it satisfying when completed. The more a habit becomes part of your life the less motivation is needed.

CHAPTER 16

HOW TO STICK WITH GOOD HABITS EVERY DAY

It is satisfying to make progress, and it is important to provide visual evidence of progress as they reinforce behavior and add a bit of immediate satisfaction to the activity. Visual measure comes in many forms but the most effective is the habit tracker.

HOW TO KEEP YOUR HABIT ON TRACK

The habit track is a simple way to measure whether a habit is done or not, the most basic is to use a calendar to cross off whether a habit is done or not.

Many people have successfully tracked their habits. The most famous being Benjamin Franklin, who, at the age of twenty, started carrying a booklet everywhere, tracking about thirteen personal virtues.

Habit tracking is very powerful. This is because it makes a behavior obvious, attractive, and satisfying. A few benefits will include:

HABIT TRACKING IS OBVIOUS

Recording actions creates triggers that initiate the next action. Most people have a distorted view of their own behavior, so habit tracking keeps you honest. Because when there is an evidence, it is usually impossible to lie.

Research has shown that most people who track their progress on goals like weight loss, lowering blood pressure, quitting smoking, and so on, are more likely to improve than those who do not.

HABIT TRACKING IS ATTRACTIVE

The most efficient form of motivation is when there is obvious progress. When there is a signal of progress, anyone will be motivated to continue on the same path. In a small way, habit tracking can have an addictive effect on motivation; each small win feeds your desire to be successful.

HABIT TRACKING IS SATISFYING

This is the most important of all. It is satisfying to cross items off your to-do list. It feels very good to watch your result grow: if it feels good, that is a cue that triggers endurance.

It helps people to keep eyes on the prize. It helps people to be focused on the process rather than the result. It provides visual that an individual is casting votes for the type of person he wants to become.

Tracking isn't for everyone, but almost everyone can benefit from it. Tracking can be made easier when measurement is automated and manual tracking limited to most important habits. Record every habit when they occur; completion of every habit is the cue to write down.

WHAT CAN WE DO TO MAKE TRACKING EASIER?

First, whenever possible, measurement should be automated. Once you know where to get the data entry, add a note to your calendar to review it each week or each month; which is more practical than daily.

Second, manual tracking should be limited to your most important habits. It is better to track consistently then track sporadically.

Last, record each measurement immediately after the habits occurs: try habit stacking + habit tracking. Example, when I hang up the phone from a sales call, I will move one paper clip over. Or after I put my plate in the dishwasher, I will write down what I ate.

HOW TO RECOVER QUICKLY WHEN HABITS BREAK DOWN

It is inevitable for habits not to be interrupted no matter how consistent a person is. There is one simple rule: Never miss twice.

The first mistake is never the one that ruins you but a spiral of subsequent mistakes. Missing one habit is accidental but missing it twice is the start of a new one; this distinguishes winners from losers.

KNOWING WHEN (AND WHEN NOT) TO TRACK A HABIT

Usually, the disadvantage of tracking habits is that we become driven by numbers rather than the purpose behind the numbers.

A person can begin to focus on working long hours over working for meaningful hours. It is very important to keep habits in perspective; not just for the numbers but the evidence you are actually moving in the right direction and a brief moment of immediate pleasure for a job well done.

CHAPTER 17

HOW AN ACCOUNTABILITY PARTNER CAN CHANGE
EVERYTHING

Just as people are more likely to repeat an experience when the end is satisfying and avoid it when the end is painful, the costlier a mistake is the faster a person will learn from it. The more the immediate pain, the less likely the behavior.

Bad habits are repeated because they serve in a way, which are difficult to abandon. Behavior changes when there is an immediate consequence. For instance, students show up in class when grades are tied to attendance.

Pain is an effective teacher, if failure is painful then it gets fixed. The best way to overcome this is to increase the speed of the punishment associated with the behavior.

There is definitely a limit to this use. If punishment is going to be relied upon to change any behavior, the strength of the punishment must match the relative strength of the behavior it is trying to correct. For instance, to exercise the cost of laziness must be more than the cost of exercise. Behavior will shift if the punishment is painful enough and reliably enforced.

THE HABIT CONTRACT

To make bad habit unsatisfying the best way is to make them painful at the moment, using a habit contract could help. Most times knowing that someone is watching is enough motivation and this process can be automated.

We always want to present ourselves as perfect to the world; because it will get positive reaction from others or make them like us. This is why getting an accountability partner or signing a habit contract works so well. Even if you don't want to create a full-blown contract, simply having an accountability partner can be useful.

ADVANCED TACTICS

HOW TO GO FROM BEING MERELY GOOD TO

BEING TRULY GREAT

CHAPTER 18

THE TRUTH ABOUT TALENT

(WHEN GENES MATTER AND WHEN THEY DON'T)

Many people know Michael Phelps, he has won more medals not only more than any swimmer but also more than any Olympian in any sport.

Hicham El Guerrouj was a Moroccan runner. For many years he held the record in the mile, fifteen hundred meter, and two thousand meter. He won gold in the fifteen hundred meter and five thousand meter races at the Olympic games in Athens, Greece, in 2004.

Imagine they were to switch sports. It would be impossible for both to do as well as they have in their field based on body composition.

One ultimate secret to maximizing odds of success is to choose the right field of competition. Like Michael Phelps in the pool or Hicham El Guerrouj on the track, you want to play a game where the odds are in your favor.

To embrace this strategy is to embrace the fact that people are born with different abilities. Many people don't like to discuss this fact. This is not the extreme of biological determinism. Where it seems like some are destined for failure and others doomed for failure. But people must understand that the strength of genes is the weakness that can't easily be changed; being six feet tall is useful for basketball.

The people at the top of any competitive field are not only well trained, they are suited for the task. That is why to be truly great, selecting the right place to focus is crucial.

Genes do not determine destiny but areas of opportunity. They predispose but do not predetermine.

HOW YOUR PERSONALITY INFLUENCES YOUR HABITS

Genes operate beneath every habit and behavior. Everyone's unique cluster of traits predispose him to a particular personality. Genes have been shown to influence everything a person does. There is a strong genetic tendency to how obedient or rebellious a person is when facing authority.

Personality is a set of characteristics consistent from time to time. The most proven scientific analysis of personality trait is the Big Five; broken down to five spectrums of behavior.

1. Openness to experience: curious and inventive to cautious and consistent.
2. Conscientiousness: organized and efficient to easygoing and spontaneous.

3. Extroversion: outgoing and energetic to solitary and reserved.

4. Agreeableness: friendly and compassionate to challenging and detached.

5. Neuroticism: anxious and sensitive to confident, calm and stable.

All these five characteristics have biological underpinning. Extroversion for instance, can be tracked from birth. Babies who go toward loud noise were more likely to be extroverts than babies who ran away from it.

Habits are usually determined by personalities. So, the major focus is to build habits that work for your personality. There are versions of every habit that are enjoyable; habits need to be to stick.

People with high agreeableness are kind, considerate, and warm. They have a higher level of oxytocin and are more inclined to bond with people. They increase feelings of trust and are a natural antidepressant.

People with high neuroticism level tend to be more anxious than others and worry more naturally than others. Personalities do not solely determine habits but genes already incline people to certain things.

Deeply rooted preferences, which are a product of personality differences, make some behaviors easier for some people compared to others.

Tailoring your habits to your personality is a good start.

HOW TO FIND A GAME WHERE THE ODDS ARE IN YOUR FAVOR

Learning to play a game where the odds are in your favor is critical to maintaining motivation and feelings of success. Pick the right habit and the process is easy, pick the wrong one and life is a struggle.

The real truth is, in theory, you can enjoy almost anything, but in practice, you are more likely to enjoy things that come more naturally to you. People who seem to be talented in a particular area may receive praise and accolades for doing a good job in the area, which in turn keeps them energized to make progress where others have failed.

To discover where is best. The most common strategy is trial and error but life is short, right? There is a better way. It is called the explore/exploit trade off. It is a period of exploration, called dating in relationships, and split testing in business.

The goal is to try out many possibilities; research a wide range of ideas. Shift focus to the solution you have found, keep experimenting occasionally. If you are winning you exploit, exploit, exploit but if you're losing explore, explore, explore.

This optimal approach depends on how much time you have. If you have time explore well, then exploit.

To explore these different options, there are a series of questions you can ask yourself:

- *What feels like fun to me, but work to others?*
- *What makes me lose track of time?*
- *What do I get greater returns than the average person?*
- *What comes naturally to me?*

However, some of these just come by luck. Should we leave it to luck then? Definitely not. If you can't win by being better, you can win by being different.

With the combination of skills, the level of competition is reduced which makes it easier to stand out. Specialization is a powerful way to overcome the "accident" of bad genetics. The more you master a skill, the harder it becomes for others to compete with you.

Boiling water could soften a potato and harden an egg, you can't tell which you are but you can play a game where it is better to be hard or soft. If you discover a more suitable condition, you can transform the situation from one where the odds are against you to where it favors you.

HOW TO GET THE MOST OUT OF YOUR GENES

Our genes don't eliminate the need for hard work, it clarifies it. They tell us where to work hard. Once we realize our strength, we know where to spend our time and energy on. The better a person understands his nature, the better his strategy can be.

Genes can't make anyone successful if the work is not done. So, the best way to ensure habits remain satisfying over the long run is to pick behaviors that align with personality and skill. Work hard on the things that come easy.

Biological differences matter a lot, but it is more productive to fulfil your own potential than comparing yourself to someone else. The point is not the natural limit. It has nothing to do with reaching the zenith of your capabilities. Many people get so immersed in this lie that they fail to lift a finger and exert the necessary effort to break forth.

CHAPTER 19

THE GOLDILOCKS RULE: HOW TO STAY MOTIVATED IN LIFE AND WORK

The human mind loves challenges but only when they are within an optimal zone of manageable difficulty. The goldilocks rule states that humans experience peak motivation when working on tasks that are right on the edge of their current abilities. Not too hard. Not too easy. Just right.

After the establishment of a habit, it is important to continue to make advancement even in small ways. Improvement requires a delicate balance.

When a new good habit begins to emerge, it is better to keep it as easy as possible so it can stick. The little improvements and new challenges will keep you engaged and you will hit the flow state, which is the experience of being "in the zone" and fully immersed in an activity.

Improvement usually requires a balance. Everyone needs the challenge that pushes them to the edge while continuing to make progress, which is enough to stay motivated. Behavior needs to be challenging to keep it satisfying.

Mastery requires practice, but the more the practice the more boring that routine becomes. Once there has been a level of gain, interest begins to wane, sometimes it even happens faster than that.

The greatest threat to success is not failure but boredom. People usually get bored with habits and just quit, and progress is hindered. This is the reason many habit-forming products are those that provide continued form of novelty.

Porn provides sexual novelty, junk food provides culinary novelty, and so on. They all have a degree of surprise continuously. This is known as the variable reward in psychology.

No habit will stay interesting forever. At some point, everyone faces the same challenge on the journey of self-improvement. There will be days when no one is motivated to work, but the ability to hang in there amidst the boredom is what shows the difference between a professional and an amateur.

Professionals will stick to the schedule while amateurs run away. Professional takes action even when the mood isn't right. To be excellent, a man must just fall in love with doing the same thing over and over.

CHAPTER 20

THE DOWNSIDE OF CREATING GOOD HABITS

Habits create the foundation for mastery, and the benefit of these habits come at a cost. When you want to maximize potential and attain mastery, you will need to combine automatic habits and deliberate practice.

In chess, when the basic movements of the pawns, knights, and all have become automatic, then the player can focus on the next level of the game.

Each chunk of information that is committed to memory opens up the mental space for more effortful thinking. This is true for general endeavor.

When the single details have been known so well that an individual can now do them without thinking then he can begin to focus on advanced details.

An individual will attain Mastery when he narrows his focus to a tiny element of success repeating it until he internalizes the skill.

The good part of habit formation is that things can be done without thinking but the downside of habits is that you get used to doing things a certain way then stop paying attention.

Gaining experience may seem like a sign of getting better but it is not the same. Most times when a skill has been mastered, there is usually a slight decline over time. To achieve elite level of performance the individual must combine habits and practice, deliberately.

MASTERING ONE HABIT

To attain mastery, an individual must avoid slipping in to complacency but establish a system for reflection and review. An individual must continue to refine and improve.

HOW TO REVIEW YOUR HABITS AND MAKE ADJUSTMENTS

Reflection and review enable the long-term improvement of all habits because it makes an individual aware of his mistakes and helps to consider paths of improvement. Improvement is not just about learning habits, it is about fine-tuning them.

Reflection provides a sense of perspective; daily habits are powerful because of how they compound. Periodic reflection and review is like reviewing oneself in a mirror.

Top performers in all fields engage in various types of reflection and review, and the process need not be so complicated.

Gold medal swimmer Katie Ledecky, records her health level, nutrition, and sleep.

Chris Rock does the same during and after every show, taking down notes of killer lines and where he needs to make adjustments.

Business moguls and investors keep business journals to record and track their decisions weekly.

To do that efficiently, you can keep a weekly or monthly review of your progress, and also an integrity report, where one could note mistakes and help get back on track.

Reflection also brings a sense of perspective. Habits done daily are powerful because of how they compound. Never reviewing habits is like never looking in the mirror, with consistent review you will be sure to be on the right track.

Ultimately, reflection and review offer an ideal time to analyze one of the valid aspects of behavior change: Identity.

HOW TO BREAK BELIEFS THAT HOLD YOU BACK

Repeating a habit is essential to building up evidence of desired identity. The more deeply an idea is tied to us, the stronger we will defend it.

The very key to reduce loss of identity is to redefine oneself as such that important aspects of the individual's identity is kept, even if role changes.

Habits can lock us into our previous pattern of thinking and acting, even when the world is shifting. Everything is not permanent. Life itself is constantly changing.

Reflection and review are the antidote to the poison of self-awareness

The tighter we cling to an identity the harder it is to grow beyond it. When properly chosen, an identity can be flexible rather than fixed. Identity progresses with the change of circumstances, rather than against.

Life changes constantly, so need to periodically check to see if old habits and beliefs are still serving.

CONCLUSION

The secret to results that can last

There is an old Greek parable: Sorites Paradox. Which talks about the effect one small action can have when it is repeated long enough.

No one can be rich unless you pile one coin, then another, and another.

Habit change is a function of thousands of one percent improvement stacked up, with each being a fundamental unit of the whole system.

Just as one coin won't make an individual rich, the same can be said that thirty minutes of exercise or a page a day reading is unlikely to deliver any notable change. Most times, small improvements are discarded because they seem meaningless, but gradually the scale of life starts to move as an individual continues to lay a small change on top of another.

Success shouldn't be seen as a goal to reach; it is a system to improve, an endless process to refine.

If an individual is having problems changing their habits, the problem is not them but the system. The secret to getting results that last is to never stop making daily improvements.

In this book, stories about top performers in several fields, Olympic and Gold medalists, award-winning artists, business leaders, and many others, have all made use of the science of small habits to master their craft and push their way to the top of their field.

Many of them go through different circumstance and overcome obstacles but ultimately progressed in the same way: through a commitment to tiny, sustainable, unrelenting improvements.

Habit formation is continuous. There is no finish line or a permanent solution. No matter what you are looking to improve, keep the laws in focus and look for the next one percent improvement.

The secret to getting results that last is to never stop making improvements. Just don't stop!

You can build a great business, just don't stop!

You can have a great body, just don't stop!

You can be highly knowledgeable, just don't stop!

Small habits compound, they don't add up.

This is the power of the atomic habits. Tiny changes. Remarkable results.

Made in the USA
Columbia, SC
15 January 2020